Pet Trusts

Yes for the Dog

Pauline G. Dembicki

Attorney at Law

Cover Art Gad Savage

First Edition

This book is intended as information about our legal system and is not intended as legal advice. Please talk to your attorney before establishing your estate plan. Laws vary among states and countries.

Dedication

This book is dedicated to:

Chichi

Elvis

Rudy

Ziggy

Perky (multiples)

Baby

Steve and Eddie and

vicariously Dot.

Pet Trusts

Yes for the Dog

Pauline G. Dembicki
Attorney at Law

Author Forward

After practicing law for almost thirty years, I see my work falling into two categories: planning and crisis management.

Planning is less expensive, has more options and less aggravation. It's a great way to protect your assets, decisions and loved ones. Today, with one of the largest pet populations in U.S. history, we are planning for care of our pets if they outlive us.

To demystify and encourage estate planning, I lecture to community groups, explaining the options you have, e.g. wills, trusts, pre-nuptial agreements, powers of attorney and more. At each lecture I caution the audience that my words of wisdom are not legal advice but general information about our legal system.

This book is not legal advice. It's general information about our legal system for you to consider before you meet with your lawyer.

Legal advice happens when you meet with a lawyer individually and agree to work together. There is usually a written agreement that describes the work anticipated, the cost and when payment is due.

The main chapter of this book is about pet trusts in Illinois. The full text of the Illinois law is at the back of the book and there is a chapter on finding a lawyer. There is a list of the states in the U.S. that have pet trust laws. Many countries, including England, have pet trust laws.

At the end of this book is my law dictionary as a reference.

An Introduction to Planning Issues

Estate plans are instructions about who will inherit your property (valuables) after you pass away. They include plans for disability, for instance, powers of attorney for health care and property and trusts.

Pet trusts are plans for your pet if you become ill or disabled and cannot continue the day to day responsibilities of caring for your pet. They provide a plan if your pet outlives you. Some pet trusts are very complex while others are alarmingly simple.

My introduction to pet trusts came when my friend Martha made "arrangements" for her cat if the cat outlived her. Her cousin agreed to adopt Blackeye, and Martha set aside money for the care of the cat. Martha made a simple joint tenancy bank account with her cat cousin. She deposited money into the account to cover food, veterinary visits and toys for the cat. There was extra money to pay the cousin for her kindness. Martha didn't tell the cousin about the amount in the account.

After Martha died, her cousin picked up the cat. When the executor of Martha's estate went through her paperwork, she found the joint tenancy account and delivered it to the cat cousin. There is no word on how this is working out. Still the cat hasn't been calling my office.

In 2005, the Illinois legislature enacted a Pet Trust law. The text is in the back of the book.

The soft underbelly of the Pet Trust is that your pet can't speak up if things aren't working as you planned them. Martha's plan was based on trust. Will you fly on faith or have checks and balances? Is there enough money involved? Each trust will be a little different.

While trusts are designed to operate out of court, some are challenged with lawsuits. The challengers tend to be relatives who think they should have inherited the money set aside for the dog, cat or horse. They are sometimes called greedy relatives.

Chapter Organization

The main chapter of this book begins with definitions and goals. They are followed by a series of questions and answers about pet trusts and a review.

The full text of the Illinois Pet Trust law is in the book along with a list of the states that have Pet Trust laws in the U.S. Many countries, including England, have laws to cover pet trusts.

At the end of the book is Pauline's Law Dictionary containing the words and phrases from the chapters of this book and a few more.

This book is deliberately short so it can be read in a few hours to pull the bandage off and get you started to get your affairs in order for your pet.

Pet Trusts

In this chapter you will learn:

Who can make a pet trust;

Where your original pet trust document should be stored;

How much should be put into your pet trust, and

Eighteen new words.

Pet Trust Terminology

Beneficiary - the person(s), or entity (e.g. charity) that receives something under the terms of your will or trust.

Caregiver – the person who has physical custody of and is responsible for the day to day care of your pet.

Successor caregiver – the person who has physical custody of and is responsible for the day to day care of your pet in the instance the first named caregiver is unable to act.

Estate – the valuables in your name alone, including personal property (e.g. bank accounts, jewelry, cars, stock) and real property (houses, condominiums and castles).

Executor – the person nominated in your will to carry out the terms of the document.

Heir – the person or persons who will receive your estate if you do not make a will, or if part or all of your will fails. Heirs are determined under state law as of the date of your death.

Intestate – a person who does not have a will.

Legatee – the person(s) or entity who receives something under the terms of your will.

Pet Trust – a set of instructions about the care of your pet if you become disabled or if your pet outlives you.

Successor executor – the second or third person in line nominated to carry out the terms of your will.

Successor trustee – the second or third person in line nominated to carry out the terms of your trust.

Testamentary capacity – the ability to understand what you own (your estate) and to recognize your friends and family.

Testate – a person who has a will.

Testator – the person making a will.

Trust – a way of holding property. There are many kinds of trusts.

Trustee – the person who holds and distributes the money in the trust according to the instructions.

Will – a set of written instructions stating who will inherit your estate. A will nominates an executor and successor executor.

Witnesses – the people who see you sign your will, powers of attorney, trust(s) or other documents, who believe you are of sound mind and memory.

What is a pet trust?

A pet trust is a set of written instructions stating who will care for your pet and who will manage the money to care for your pet if the pet outlives you or if you are unable to continue to care for your pet during your lifetime. In many pet trusts, one person will handle the money and take care of your pet.

Who can make a pet trust?

In Illinois, you must be at least 18 years old and of sound mind and memory to make a will. The same rule applies to making a pet trust.

What is testamentary capacity?

Testamentary capacity is sometimes called sound mind and memory. It means that you understand what you own and who your family and friends are. It means that the division of your property was your idea and not one foisted upon you by another person. There are individuals who feel that leaving money to the dog is not something done with a sound mind.

What law controls Pet Trusts?

State law covers pet trusts, in Illinois the Pet Trust law is in the Trusts and Fiduciaries Act at 760 ILCS 5/15/2. Through the date of publication, there are no cases at the appeal level on Pet Trusts in Illinois. The statute is in the appendix of this book.

Your Pet Trust should be prepared with respect to the state where you live.

Currently forty states have Pet Trust laws. England and many other countries have Pet Trust Laws.

Are you required to hire an attorney to prepare your Pet Trust?

No, you are not required to use an attorney to prepare your pet trust; however, it's a really good idea. The law took effect in 2005, and is still relatively new. An estate planner should be able to help you with the options available.

Can you put a provision for the care of your pet in your last will and testament?

Yes, provisions for your pet can be a part of your will. If you do that, it is called a testamentary trust.

What is a testamentary trust?

A testamentary (pet) trust is created in your will and takes effect after you die. One of the drawbacks is that the trust will not be funded until your estate passes through probate. If you get a new pet, you will need to update your will. This approach does not have instructions for the care of your pet if you are temporarily or permanently unable to care for your pet during your lifetime.

Are there other options?

A second option is a trust document that only addresses the care of your pet. It includes the designation of caregiver and trustee, disposition of your pet's remains, and disposition of any money remaining in the trust after the pet dies. This could be as simple as a one or two page document.

There are different options for funding that your attorney can explain to you.

What is funding?

Funding is when money is deposited into the trust. It can be done after the trust is created or at another time certain, e.g. the date of your death. Talk to your attorney about the options.

Is either option better?

Both options provide protection for your pets. The testamentary trust will only operate after you die, has no provisions for the care of your pet if you are ill or unable to care for the pet during your lifetime, and funds may not be immediately available to care for your pet.

If you want or need to make changes to a testamentary trust, you will need to revise your will.

A trust that only addresses the care of your pet is easier to change if your pet(s) change.

The option that is best for you will depend on your decisions and circumstances.

When is a testamentary trust funded?

A testamentary trust is created in your will and may (depending on your estate) go through the probate court. Funds may not be immediately available unless you make provisions to make money available sooner. Talk to your attorney.

What happens if I am ill or hospitalized and can't take care of my pet on a temporary basis?

You can build provisions into your pet trust to cover this contingency. Talk to your attorney.

How will people know I have a pet trust?

Before creating a pet trust, you should discuss your plan with the potential trustee and caregivers. Explain what you want and ask if they are willing to step up to the litter box if needed. Assuming you have regular contact with the trustee, they will likely be told if you are ill or dead.

This discussion can include information about the location of the pet's veterinary records, food allergies, diets, preferences and supplements.

You can make a wallet card that has contact information for your caretaker and trustee. First responders may look for emergency identification and can contact your people. Your attorney's name and contact information should be on the card.

What does a pet trustee really do?

In most cases, the trustee will take possession of your dear pets and hunt for the account, trust agreement or talk to the lawyer. Most pet trusts will only have one person who handles the kibble and the doggie. They should follow the instructions in the trust. The pet trustee may interact with your executor or trustee of a trust made for your benefit.

Someone needs access to your home in case of an emergency. The trustee needs the name and contact information of your veterinarian, the location of your pet's medical records and any special instructions as to food or diet.

Dusty Springfield left money for her cat's care. She directed the cat to sleep on (not in) one of her nightgowns, eat imported baby food for a year and be played Dusty Springfield music before bedtime.

Who can you nominate as trustee?

When selecting a caregiver, think about people who already know your pet. It should be a person over 18 years of age. Ask the potential caregiver if they are willing to accept the responsibility and whether or not they want a fee. The fee should be specifically drafted into the agreement.

Does the trustee have to make reports on the trust?

The Illinois Pet Trust Act does not require the trustee to make reports. Depending on the size and complexity of the trust, you may want to require that records of some type be maintained. You may also want to designate a person to review the records.

Does the trustee get paid?

This varies from trust to trust. Talk to your potential trustee and ask if they expect a fee. If the answer is yes, you need to add funds (and language) to cover their fee. It could be an annual fee or a onetime fee.

Does the caregiver get a fee?

Ask potential caregivers if they want to be paid. If they do, this number needs to be factored into the amount of money set aside for your pet. The trust needs language to address this provision.

If there isn't one person I trust completely, can I nominate two people to act together as trustee?

This depends on the size of your trust, your pet's anticipated lifespan and the standard of living you describe in your pet trust. As a general rule, it's better to nominate one person and a second to act in succession (one person after the other) to care for your pet. The other option is one person to handle the money and another to take care of your pet.

Can I rely on one person to take care of my pet and handle the money?

Yes, one person can wear both hats and be responsible for handling the money and taking care of Spot. You should nominate a second caretaker in the event the first is unavailable or unable to take care of your pet.

Unless you are filthy rich or a Hollywood star, your trust is likely to have one person taking care of the pet who also handles the money. The amount in most pet trusts for one animal could be less than the cost of a new car or as little as the cost of a really cool bicycle.

What other decisions need to be made in the pet trust?

Two other decisions you need to make in the pet trust are the disposition of your pet's remains when they die and the disposition of any unspent funds in the trust.

What are unspent funds?

Unspent funds are those remaining in the trust when your pet dies. Let's imagine you have a two year old dog in relatively good health. With vet expenses, grooming, food and toys, you would set an amount to pay those costs over the anticipated lifespan of your pet. You may build in fees for the caregiver and trustee, if applicable. If your pet dies before the money is spent, you can designate where the money will go.

You could name a charity to receive the money, a person or even the caregiver. Some people feel the caregiver should not get the remainder because it would give them incentive to do evil things.

What happens if I don't name a beneficiary for any funds not spent on the care of my pet?

Illinois law has two options if you don't make a provision for the unspent funds. If you have an estate plan, the balance of the unused pet trust funds will go to the residual taker under your will or trust.

If you do not have an estate plan, the balance of the trust will pass to your heirs at law.

What happens if all the money I set aside for my pet is spent before my pet dies?

If that happens, the caregiver may be able to pay for the care of your pet. You may want another provision about custody of your pet if they cannot. You could designate someone who may be able to adopt the pet without the financial support. Have a discussion with the caregiver and an alternate pet caregiver if the money runs out.

Where should I store the original pet trust document?

The trust document needs to be stored where it is safe from inadvertent destruction and is available to the trustee if and when the time comes to apply the trust.

If I nominate someone to be a caregiver and/or trustee, are they required to act if my pet outlives me?

No, nominating a person to act as a caregiver or trustee does not create a legal obligation. That is one reason why successors are so important. A person who is ready, willing and able to get involved when you talk to them at the planning stage can have a change in circumstances when the call to action is made. The person could be ill, have moved away, live where pets are not welcome, or be otherwise unavailable to follow through with the arrangement.

If all of my nominated caregivers and trustees cannot act what happens?

You can draft in a provision for a third person to nominate someone to take care of your pet and handle the money. If no person who is nominated can serve, a court can appoint someone to act.

Can I nominate my spouse as caregiver or trustee?

While you could do this, a pet is usually owned by a family. Talk to your attorney about any special circumstances.

What is a pet trust contest?

A pet trust contest is when the validity of your trust is called into question by means of a lawsuit or threat of a lawsuit. There are at least two major areas of contest: one) when relatives or earlier beneficiaries allege there is too much money in the trust, and two) when relatives or earlier beneficiaries question your ability or competence to make the trust. Other areas of challenge include forgery and undue influence.

Who pays for a pet trust contest?

In a will or trust contest, the estate pays for defending the will or trust, generally. It is likely that the pet trust would bear the burden of defending a pet trust contest. Sadly, that reduces the amount available to care for your pet. The person(s) who challenges the trust must pay their own attorney's fees.

Will contests and trust contests are expensive. However, there is a specific provision in the Illinois pet trust law that allows a judge to reduce the amount set aside for your pet if it substantially exceeds what is needed to care for the pet. You can include a schedule of how you reached the amount of money to put into the trust as a means to support the reasonableness.

Who can challenge my pet trust?

Your heirs can challenge your pet trust. Beneficiaries under an earlier will or estate plan may challenge your pet trust.

What does it cost to prepare a Pet Trust?

While asked often, there is no way to estimate the cost until we learn what you have in mind. Most attorneys will give you an estimate of cost after they learn if you are making plans for one animal or several and whether you have great detail in mind and the amount of money that is estimated to be needed for their care.

Can a pet trust cover more than one pet?

Yes, you can cover more than one pet in a trust. However if you have different pets like one dog and a horse, separate provisions may be a better idea.

Is the money paid on a monthly basis or annually?

This is a decision that you will make when establishing the trust depending on the amount in the trust. In the Martha example, which was not a statutory pet trust, after Martha died, the money in the joint bank account technically belonged to the cat cousin. They had a handshake agreement and enforcement would be difficult.

Are these trusts complicated?

There are many variables in a pet trust. Still, most pet trusts will be simple with an amount of money set aside for your pet and few instructions.

It's your decision how much you want to put into this agreement.

A basic pet trust will nominate at least two people in succession to handle the money and care for your pet. It can include instructions about specific care, disposition of remains and disposition of unspent funds after your pet dies.

Review

A pet trust is a set of written instructions about the care of your pet if your pet outlives you or if you are unable to care for them during your lifetime. In larger trusts, one person, the trustee, holds and manages the money. A second person, the caretaker, manages the care of the day to day activities of your pet. In many trusts one person takes care of the money and your pet.

In Illinois, a pet trust must be in writing and likely will require at least one witness, the same as other trusts. If your family is particularly contentious, you may want to have more than one witness.

In your pet trust document, you will nominate one trustee and at least one successor trustee. You may nominate a caregiver and a successor caregiver.

Every pet trust should have directions of where unspent funds will go if your pet dies before the funds are exhausted. Care should be taken to not put too much money in the trust since a court can reduce the amount of the trust principal if it finds the amount is more than what is needed for the care of your pet.

Keeping your will, pet trust or trust up to date, maintaining an up to date list of assets and protecting the original documents are vital to success. If you adopt a new pet, you may update your pet trust.

You are not required to hire an attorney to prepare your estate planning documents, but it is a really good idea. Remember if you make your own documents, the first time a professional (a judge or attorney) will read your documents will be after your death. At that point errors may increase costs and if the errors are big ones, your estate plan could be determined to be invalid.

How to Find a Lawyer

There are many ways to find a lawyer. You can attend lectures, read books, surf the internet or ask your friends and neighbors for names. If you have worked with an attorney on another matter, they likely will have names of estate planners and probate attorneys.

Lawyers usually practice in specific areas of law. The days of the general practitioner are fading. Thus, you will need someone who is familiar with estate law.

Once you have a name (or two) you can do an internet search to learn a little about the attorney.

Most lawyers will meet with you for a half-hour or an hour at a reduced hourly charge or no charge. This is an opportunity for the lawyer to determine whether they can accept your case and for you to determine whether or not you want to work with the lawyer.

It's important you locate a lawyer who does the kind of work you require. You probably don't want to see a criminal defense attorney to prepare a will or pet trust. As an estate planner who does probate, elder law and guardianship, I don't need to meet with someone who is charged with a felony or misdemeanor.

If your attorney does not practice the area of law that you need, ask if they can give you a name or names of attorneys who do.

Selecting an attorney includes finding one that you can speak to honestly. By revealing your family interactions, you can help the lawyer guide you through the options available. Remember, no plan is guaranteed.

If you want to make a pet trust, calculate the annual costs of care of your pet. Estimate your pet's lifespan (your veterinarian may help or you might want to do a little internet research). Talk to potential caregivers and trustees before you nominate them in estate planning documents. Be certain that you sufficiently identify your pet in the trust. Consider who will inherit any unspent trust funds after your pet dies.

Your attorney can tell you who may inherit your estate if you do not make a will. This is an educated guess since heirs are not determined until you pass away. Those same persons can challenge your pet trust.

Consider updating or making a plan to take care of you if you are unable to take care of yourself (e.g. powers of attorney, trusts). Also consider making a will or trust to distribute your property after you pass away.

Most attorneys operate with a written fee agreement. It sets out what is included. It should include the price, or how it will be calculated. It will indicate when the fee is due in part or in whole. It will say whether it is a flat fee or whether it will be billed on an hourly basis. If you make many changes after your documents are prepared, you will likely incur extra charges.

If you have questions about the agreement, ask before you sign.

You have to make the attorney selection to match your values and personality. Your decision should be based on the impression the lawyer communicates about their ability to represent you.

Ask the attorney how many cases they have handled in the particular area of law at hand. Ask for a resume. References are a slippery slope because we are required to maintain client confidentiality.

Good attorneys come in all shapes, sizes and ages. Their offices are large, small and in between. They have offices in large metropolitan areas, the suburbs, in shared office space and in their homes. They have a huge office staff and work alone. They graduated from IIT, the University of Illinois, Harvard or Georgetown. They have fancy office machines and the brand name from big box stores.

The decision is ultimately yours.

The Illinois Pet Trust

Illinois Statute 760 ILCS 5/15/2:

(a) A trust for the care of one or more designated domestic or pet animals is valid. The trust terminates when no living animal is covered by the trust. A governing instrument shall be liberally construed to bring the transfer within this Section, to presume against a merely precatory or honorary nature of its disposition, and to carry out the general intent of the transferor. Extrinsic evidence is admissible in determining the transferor's intent.

(b) A trust for the care of one or more designated domestic or pet animals is subject to the following provisions:

(1) Except as expressly provided otherwise in the instrument creating the trust, no portion of the principal or income of the trust may be converted to the use of the trustee or to a use other than for the trust's purposes or for the benefit of a covered animal.

(2) Upon termination, the trustee shall transfer the unexpended trust property in the following order:

(A) as directed in the trust instrument;

(B) if there is no such direction in the trust instrument and if the trust was created in a non-residuary clause in the transferor's will, then under the residuary clause in the transferor's will; or

(C) if no taker is produced by the application of subparagraph (A) or (B), then to the transferor's heirs, determined according to Section 2-1 of the Probate Act of 1975.

(3) The intended use of the principal or income may be enforced by an individual designated for that purpose in the trust instrument or, if none, by an individual appointed by a court having jurisdiction of the matter and parties, upon petition to it by an individual.

(4) Except as ordered by the court or required by the trust instrument, no filing, report, registration, periodic accounting, separate maintenance of funds, appointment, or fee is required by reason of the existence of the fiduciary relationship of the trustee.

(5) The court may reduce the amount of the property transferred if it determines that the amount substantially exceeds the amount required for the

intended use. The amount of the reduction, if any, passes as unexpended trust property under paragraph (2).

(6) If a trustee is not designated or no designated trustee is willing and able to serve, the court shall name a trustee. The court may order the transfer of the property to another trustee if the transfer is necessary to ensure that the intended use is carried out, and if a successor trustee is not designated in the trust instrument or if no designated successor trustee agrees to serve and is able to serve. The court may also make other orders and determinations as are advisable to carry out the intent of the transferor and the purpose of this Section.

(7) The trust is exempt from the operation of the common law rule against perpetuities.

CREDIT(S)

P.A. 78-625, § 15.2, added by P.A. 93-668, § 5, eff. Jan. 1, 2005

U.S. States with Pet Trust Laws

Note: laws change every day. Check with an attorney to see which law applies to you.

Alabama

Alaska

Arizona

Arkansas

California

Colorado

Connecticut

Delaware

District of Columbia

Georgia

Florida

Hawaii

Idaho (purpose trust)

Illinois

Indiana

Kansas

Maine

Maryland

Michigan

Missouri

Montana

Nebraska

Nevada

New Hampshire

New Jersey

New York

Pennsylvania

Rhode Island

South Carolina

South Dakota

Tennessee

Texas

Utah

Vermont

Virginia

Washington

Wisconsin

Wyoming

PAULINE'S LAW DICTIONARY

Administrator – the person nominated by heirs to carry out the administration of an estate when there is no will.

Administratrix – a female administrator.

Administrator With the Will Annexed – the person who administers a will when no named executor is able to serve; administrator w/w/a.

Beneficiary - the person, persons or entity (e.g. charity) who receive something under the terms of your will or trust.

Caregiver – the person who has physical custody of your pet and is responsible for day to day care.

Successor Caregiver – the second person nominated to have physical custody of your pet, responsible for day to day care if the first named person cannot act.

Decedent – the dead person.

Estate – the valuables in your name, including personal property (e.g. bank accounts, jewelry, cars, stock) and real property (houses, condominiums and castles).

Executor – the person nominated in your will to carry out the terms of the will.

Heir – the person or persons who will receive your estate if you do not make a will, or if part or all of your will fails. Heirs are determined under state law as of the date of your death.

Intestate – a person who does not have a will.

Lawyer – the professional who prepares your will.

Legatee – the person(s) or entity that receives something under the terms of your will.

Pet Trust – a written set of instructions about the care of your pet in the event you are unable to care for her due to illness or death.

Probate – the process of paying your final bills and delivering your estate to your beneficiaries.

Probate Court – the court that handles administration of decedent's estates and settles disputes when needed.

Successor executor – the second or third person nominated to carry out the terms of your will.

Successor trustee – the second or third person nominated to carry out the terms of your trust.

Testamentary capacity – the ability to understand what you own (your estate), to recognize the objects of your bounty and to make a division of property that you establish.

Testate – a person who has a will.

Testator – the person making the will.

Will – a set of written instructions stating who will inherit from your estate. A will also nominates an executor and successor executor.

Witnesses – the people who see you sign your will, powers of attorney, trust or other document, who believe you are of sound mind.

Epilogue

Making an estate plan (powers of attorney, wills, trusts, pet trusts) is difficult for many reasons; including cost, thinking about death or illness and realizing you will not live forever.

With planning, however, the costs are lower and the chances that your decisions will be honored are greater.

I wrote this book to show you planning isn't very difficult and the trend is to not only plan for your friends and family, but to plan for your pets.

Pet trusts are relatively new and what the courts will do with challenges to the pet trusts is uncertain. I encourage you to talk to a lawyer to set up a plan that will provide you with peace of mind.

Not having a plan for your pet isn't the end of the world. In many families, someone immediately takes steps to protect your pet. The same people often want to adopt them. It is an option for you to set up something to at least defray costs for any chewed furniture.

Thank you.

Pauline G. Dembicki

Author Biography

Pauline G. Dembicki is a graduate of IIT Kent College of Law in Chicago, Illinois. She has practiced law in Evanston, Illinois, for nearly thirty years. Her major areas of practice include estate planning, probate, elder law, trust and guardianship administration as well as contested estates in related areas of law. Pauline is appointed by the court as a guardian ad litem in adult guardianship and decedents estates.

Pauline has lectured, published, been a member and received awards from the following legal organizations: American Bar, Chicago Bar, Illinois State Bar, North Suburban Bar, Advocates Society, Illinois Institute for Continuing Legal Education, Chicago Volunteer Legal Services and the Women's Bar Association of Illinois. She is a past president of North Suburban Bar Association.

Her lecture and publication topics include wills, probate, guardianship, powers of attorney, the surrogate health care act, networking through bar organizations, trusts, land trusts, joint tenancies and many articles on appellate cases.

Ms. D. has published over a hundred articles for attorneys on estate law and over seventy-five articles for the public on estate planning. Ms. Dembicki has written three moot court plays produced at Anixter Center. She is a participant in many Law Day activities.

You can contact Ms. Dembicki at: Pauline@PaulineLaw.com

Other books by Pauline G. Dembicki

Powers of Attorney: Health Care, Property - a kindle eBook:

http://www.amazon.com/Powers-Attorney-Health-Property-ebook/dp/B00AWE0IS8

The Powers of Attorney book contains detailed information about why and how a power of attorney for health care and for property are created and the purposes, uses and limitations of powers of attorney.

Wills, Probate and Executors: Not All Evil, a kindle eBook:

http://www.amazon.com/Wills-Probate-Executors-Evil-ebook/dp/B00C7WOA5U

This book describes wills and the decisions you can and cannot make with a will. It looks at the practical positive points of probate court as well as the disadvantages. This book describes the various responsibilities of executors.

In 2013, additional books will be released on Kindle including the updated edition of Wills and *Trusts, and Powers, Oh My!* Chapters include: Wills, Inter Vivos Trusts, Living Trusts, Land Trusts, Transfer on Death Deed, Pet Trusts, Guardianship, Probate, Joint Tenancies, Health Care and Property Powers of attorney, Ways to Hold Title to Property and more.

Send an email to: book@paulinelaw.com for notice when new books are available.

Thank you. If you loved this book, please consider a short review on Amazon.com on the book page.

Made in United States
Orlando, FL
16 October 2025

70874048R00039